How Western Civilization

is Saved

By Islam

Educative Informations that you shouldn't afford to miss

Pharm. M.A Gachi

Speech by Professor Roy Casagranda

Table of Contents

1. Introduction to Civilization

2. Call for Christianity Modification

3. Western Civilization

4. Identity is essential

5. What make the west and non-west?

6. The Great Library

7. Manifestation of Islam

8. Destruction of the Book

9. Question and Answers

10. Conclusion

11. Jorting   Space

Preface

This book is a Speech of Professor Roy, I took it upon myself to make it a book for it to be an educative information especially to those who were brainwashed by media that Islam contained terrorism, don't respect females and sort of propaganda.

After studying this book, you will come to understand that Islam promote Peace and Islam never spreads by sword.

You will come to understand that muslims way of conquering in those days of Wars never including Brutality, but peaceful making, nation builders through knowledge and also socially sound by good behaviors and Justice to all.

What ever you see in bracket in this book is my wordings which is meant for further explanation for you to get it better.

Chapter 1

Introduction

(Civilization is the most advanced stage of human social and cultural development and organization. Without Islamic culture, Western civilization as we know it today would not exist. Why did I say so? Algebra, alchemy, artichoke, alcohol, and apricot are all words that came to the West from Arabic during the Crusades).

(Much more basic are the Indo-Arabic numerals (0-9), which substituted Roman numerals during a similar period and upset our ability to take part in science and exchange. This was made possible by the Latin discovery of Al-Khwarizmi, a Persian scholar from the ninth century whose name gives us the word algorithm).

The title of this Book is how Islam saved Western Civilization. For the record, I believe that that is a totally accurate statement, this isn't an attempt to back away from that title at all the thing I want to admit is the title of this talk is how Islam saved Western Civilization. I have nested a contradiction in the title that I'm going to show you later on purpose because I like to do things like that, it's just my nature so I just want you to know I'm admitting this right off the start um so to start this thing off though I also want to admit something else which is that I picked the title because there's a book that kind of inspired me, but the book is deeply flawed and the book is "How the Irish saved civilization" I got the book I want to say like 22 years ago and I hate doing this because I feel like it feels like I'm picking on somebody but the book is deeply flawed. it's riddled with two contradictions in fact and the reason I'm bringing this off is because those are some of the contradictions I want to tease out in this talk. So here's the premise of the book, in September 4, 476 A.D the Roman Empire collapsed, it was a very sad day. There was much lamenting and then the Irish save civilization, because the Irish had already converted to Christianity and Christianity of course is the core of civilization and so the Irish went to Europe and converted those awful Pagan Germanic tribesmen to Christianity and saved civilization in the process, that's wrong on multiple levels the first and most obvious level is Rome didn't fall on September 4, 476 A.D so if the whole idea is that the Irish save civilization from collapse but it didn't collapse then were the premise is already shot out of the water who are already in trouble, Rome fell May 29 1453. it's almost a thousand years later this is this isn't a small error, this is a gigantic error so that's one problem another problem with the premise is the following, most of the Germanic tribesmen were Christian so if the Irish are converting them to Christianity that's odd, it's like when President William McKinley said we're Conquering the Philippines to make it Christian and they're you know like 80% of the Philippians population were catholic. Of course what McKinley meant was to make them Protestant but anyway that's a different story we're just going to genocide 800 000 of these folks and hopefully flip them over to Protestantism didn't work.

So the second contradiction that they're going to convert the Germanic tribesmen into Christianity is actually shockingly similar to the McKinley thing I just brought up, not all of the Germanic tribesmen had converted some of them were still Pagan but the ones that that had converted were the wrong kind of Christian that's what he really means.

Chapter 2

Call for Modifying Christianity

In 325 A.D, emperor Constantine decided that Christianity was too unwieldy of a religion, it was it was too complicated, too mysterious, there were too many moving parts and it needed to be toned down a little bit, in part to get rid of some of the contradictions like for example the Trinity it was driving everybody nuts right, how does this work? he's what ? and and so Constantine said "I want 318 of you theologians to go to Nicaea and figure out how to make Christianity into something a little bit more manageable because if Rome, Rome had already majority it was already majority Christian at that point, so if the Roman Empire is going to use Christianity as the state religion to manipulate people, we as the politicians class need to be able to know what

Christianity is. How can we manipulate people through religion if we don't understand the religion"?.

so they get together at Nicaea they come up with a solution for the Trinity. There were 30 gospels, they threw 26 away, they ordered them destroyed it didn't quite work (because) we have the other 26. Most of them were found in Egypt by a by a farmer who was in the desert digging out phosphorus and he hit a jar with his with his shovel and he heard it crack and he pulled the jar out and he saw these leather-bound books, I think I want to say it was 46, 47 and he pulls out the leather bomb books and he's like I don't know what these are but I know who will know and he was a Muslim, he went to the nearby Church, the Coptic Orthodox church and he handed them to the priests and the priests went oh! I know what these are, these are the 26 Apocrypha and the church then immediately declared it a miracle that somehow the 26 Apocrypha had survived and the Coptic Church claims that all 30 Gospels are legit and rejects the rejection of the 26 Apocrypha. **Apocrypha means wrong** right? so it rejects the wrong the Declaration that they're wrong.

About Nicaea, the 318 also had a conversation about one other problem and the problem was how to understand Christ's nature on Earth. If he was God, then how did he manage sin. For example there was a guy named Arius of

Alexandria, he was living in Alexander that's why he made his career. Arius of Alexandria went, here's my suggestion Jesus was God, pure God, total God as a result he was never tempted done, no sin. But the majority said no that's wrong, Jesus was God in a man's body. The body was tempted, therefore he did experience what it would be like to be tempted but because he was God he overcame it and there was no sin that became Orthodox Doctrine. The other part became heresy it's known as the Arian heresy.

So that's the Arian heresy, it took off in Egypt it took off in Syria and the Germanic tribesmen really liked it so that's what's being converted they're being taken away from the Arian heresy into what we would we would have considered mainstream Christianity of course in the United States the average American Christian is an Arian heretic, I can prove it to you. There is a Greek guy who wrote a book called The Last Temptation Of Christ, his name was Nikos Kazantzakis. The Last Temptation Of Christ is Orthodox Christian belief, Christ was tempted as a man but overcame it because he was God, Americans went not! when Scorsese says he turned this into a movie, The French also went not! they actually set a historical movie theater on fire while people were in it, because they couldn't believe a movie that could be this heretical could be made when the reality was they were the Heretics. That was the church's official belief.

Alright fine, these are the types of contradictions I want to tackle, the assumptions that we go into these conversations were like oh! the dramatic tribesmen are pagans and oh! right? and and the reality is it's way more complicated.

 So to do that I want to start with a definition of Western Civilization, so if you take a college level course into Western civilization and for the record uh I'm a political scientist but uh history is obviously a thing of mine and I did teach for a few years with the University of Maryland.

I did teach their Intro to a western civilization class. so I'm also telling you this as a person, as a recovering uh intro to civilization professor, usually every school is probably a little bit different because it depends on the textbook and the professor but usually the class starts in 3400 BC or if you're like me and you reject BC because it's confusing, (then) 5400 years ago. The class usually goes it depends again on the text and the professor but it usually goes to 1648 with the end of the 30 Years War which didn't end in 1648 and lasted about 50 years just for the record. Just to make things not work and then intro to Western Civ 2 usually starts in 1648 and goes to the present, which I've always thought was remarkable because it shows our bias for the Contemporary period because we're going to take 5 000 years of History 5400 years ago to 400 years ago and we're going to compress that into 16 weeks and then we're going to do three and a half centuries in 16 weeks, it seems like an unfair distribution we're literally giving the recent centuries 17 times the attention that we gave the old centuries. But okay set that aside for a moment odds are good that your professor will start this class with maybe one maybe two but probably one lecture on Mesopotamia and Sumer and then in the beginning of writing and then maybe the second lecture will briefly cover Egypt and then from there your professor is going to probably go on and spend a huge amount of time on the Greeks an enormous amount of time on the Romans and then the Middle East Middle Ages kick in maybe a lecture on the Middle Ages, they lasted a thousand years, maybe it gets a lecture and then they'll be a lecturer or two at the end of the class because the Italians go, hey I have an idea let's do the Renaissance and that's a really exciting time period and then the class ends with the start with the completion of the 30 Years War when Protestants and Catholics Slaughter each other Wholesale in Europe. The 30 years war is one of my favorite Wars because Spain and Sweden fight each other, you know what I mean they're just you almost don't need to know anything else about the war, They fought three battles in Germany the Spanish Army and the Swedish army met in Germany and then they beat the crap out of each other, for the record the swedes while they were in Germany plundered it sort of the Spanish of course you're in Germany come on Fred's gonna plunder and they stole a bunch of stuff from the city of Wurzburg and they took it back to Sweden and a bunch of that ended up in museums and the City of Wurzburg a few years ago sued Sweden to get their stuff back from 1648 and the European Union went now sorry too bad you lost it, I thought wow! why you ask, well because if Stockholm (capital of Sweden) had to return to Wurzburg's plundered Goods, then Berlin (Germany) and London would have to return to Egypt and Iraq it's plundered Goods that would have been a catastrophic event for museums in Europe, right? one of my favorite museums on the planet is the pergamon museum it's in Berlin, if you if you love anything to do with the Middle East, it is amazing you have to go to the pergamon in Berlin. They have a whole Greek temple that the Germans took out of turkey Stone by Stone, they have the gates of Babylon that they took out of Iraq Stoned by Stone and they erected erected it inside a building specifically constructed to have these two Marvels inside them and in a way I'm grateful because you can go see it, they're intact they're preserved in a way, I'm horrified because these weren't German National Treasures. I have actually been to the Temple of pergamon that's in Berlin. In Turkey I've been to pergamon and there's like you know where it is? it's like wow! so I've been to both I've seen where it's supposed to be and I've seen where it is. The reason why I'm bringing up the class is because nested in it, is a really interesting admission and then a massive omission.

Chapter 3

Western Civilization

The admission is that Western Civilization started on the banks of the Euphrates., the Tigris and the Nile and then they're never talked about again, that's it. Now obviously European civilization is amazing, I mean I'm after all speaking a European language in North America you don't get here and Conquer two whole continents with at least not having a really strong propensity to violence. You know what I mean there has to be something there, it didn't just happen, so there it's not to reject that there doesn't need to be a story about Europe. I'm a political scientist I'm not a historian, historians start in Sumer because 5400 years ago is when they mostly agree, there's a little bit of disagreement that that's when writing started what a historian is they're different from a political scientist the historian believes that

Civilization starts with writing because a historian is a literary critic who does non-fiction the difference between a historian and an English major is English Majors do fiction, historians do non-fiction so if there isn't something written there's nothing for historians to talk about. So, I think government starts civilization not writing, in fact why did writing happen in the first place? what happened was bureaucrats were trying to figure out how to keep track of how many cows they had, how much wheat they had stored in the granaries, how many swords they had, how many horses they had and they went, the politician class went to the bureaucrats and said you need to come up with some mechanism to keep track of all of this, and so the bureaucrats began coming up with symbol sets for numbers and for items and over time those symbol sets evolved into writing in other words government had to come first.

The year is 6260, according to the ancient Egyptian calendar. At some point, an ancient Egyptian politician said you know, what sucks that the farmers don't know what day to plant their crop every year, if we made a calendar and kept track of when spring started, that would really make our lives easier, in other words even the Advent of the calendar isn't the start of civilization there was a government before that, by the way just for the record the Egyptian calendar doesn't have leap years in it, so it's off by 0.24 years it's actually 0.239 I think, so in other words you need to do a leap year every four years but every 100 years you need to skip leap year but every thousand years you need to go ahead and do the leap year with a normally skipped so in the year 2000 we were supposed to skip that leap year but we weren't because it was the Thousand Year point so that was the that's why we went ahead and did it anyway really complicated but a lot of fun. The ancient Egyptians because they don't have that, their calendar is so old they're off by four years in other words a way to think of it is the first day of spring has rotated through every single day of their calendar four times, so it's really the year 6260. I'm bringing that up because what that meant then was Farmers every four years had to actually move the date one day right because the start of spring and Egyptians were like people can keep track of that let's just move on, this calendar will be to to wonky complicated otherwise. Egypt probably created government about 6500 years ago, so civilization in Egypt is probably about 6500 years old we think that the Sumerians probably started government a couple of centuries later. so the Sumerians beat Egypt to writing but the Egyptians beat Sumerians the government and the two of them were always really close to each other Whenever there was a development, so it just kept whoever was first the other guy was second Sumer in Egypt they just kept flipping back and forth in developments, so another way to look at this is Egypt was conquered by the Romans in 31 BC, this is a pretty catastrophic event for Egypt at every level infact because the Romans were rough, to give you an idea what I mean by the Romans were rough,

When Gaius Julius Caesar, conquered Gaul, today France he killed one million of the Celtic population living in Gulf. They go how bad was that exactly, he murdered one third of the population, He enslaved another million and then he turned and looked at the remaining million and went welcome to the Roman Republic.

That was the Roman way, now the Romans varied and how cruel they were so when they got to Dacia, they killed and enslaved everybody. In fact they were so thorough about destroying Dacia, you don't know where Dacia is, it's effectively been erased from history. I'll tell you where it is. It's Romania, as in the Romans erased it from existence and then named it after themselves and it still holds the new name. When the Romans conquered Egypt, they wanted to crush the Egyptian population so they did things like they banned Egyptians from owning land, they banned Egyptians from riding horses, they banned Egyptians from doing anything but wearing the color blue. Egyptians had to always wear blue, and the Romans did this because they knew that the Egyptian population was going to be complicated to rule over and then they were right, the Egyptians kept rebelling so the Romans kept massacring them by mass crucifixions, they were just crucify whole segments of the Egyptian population and then say look this is going to happen to you if you keep rebelling and of course the Egyptians just kept rebelling. So, if we decide that Egyptian civilization stopped abruptly in 31 BC, I'm happy to do that for purposes of this conversation. Then by the time it got to 31 BC Egypt civilization was 4000 years old. Another way to think of this is when Alexander the Great, conquered Egypt and went to the pyramids for the first time and gazed upon the pyramids, the Giza Pyramids which were not the oldest pyramids right? the sulcata pyramids are the oldest pyramids. The Giza Pyramids are 200 years younger. The Giza Pyramids were 2300 years old for him. When he was looking at the pyramids he was going, I can't believe this is 23 centuries old? that's so insanely ancient, he was 23 centuries ago. We are as far from Alexander the Great as the pyramids were from him. Just to give you a little sense of this, in other words one lecture on Egypt, seems probably inappropriate. One lecture on Mesopotamia probably seems like a little too much if you're admitting that's the founding of your civilization that's a really strange thing. Egypt had a civil war that won 170 years. The United States is what? 230 something depending on, do you start it with Declaration of Independence or the moment the Constitution went into effect, I've never figured out which one I want. One of those two is right.

I mean Egypt just has a sneeze that lasted almost as long as the United States has been around. I need you to re-frame the way you think about this that this civilization that was birthed in the banks of the Tigris the Euphrates and the Nile can't possibly have stopped being there. But if you've been listening to the news lately, it gets really interesting because when Russia invaded Ukraine all I hear now is Russia almost accepted Western culture, Russia almost accepted Western democracy, the West is supporting Ukraine, West West, West, it's the old conversation from the Cold War reborn again, so we got to go back a little bit here before the Cold War to understand some terminology. When the English were Conquering the world, when the English were making the world England. They didn't finish obviously, they didn't finish they got 40 percent done and and they ran out of steam. But 40 percent is amazing! think about it, that tiny, itty bitty, teeny, weeny little Island, where they boil their steak and Fry their tomatoes. Where it's always raining somehow conquered 40% of the planet, I still can't wrap my mind around it. They only ruled it for 200 years but still! I don't even know what to make of that, that's talent there was Talent there, I'm not denying the talent, just incredible talent because a lot of it wasn't violence right? the English would plant a flag and the Indians are looking at it going, what is that? it's a flag what does it do it means we conquered you and the unions are like oh crap! you mean if we had gotten to your tiny-little island and planted the Indian flag we would have conquered you? and the English were like Yep!

That's how this works, we got you. So, there was a little bit of Psyching him out right? that was also going on. So, when the English had done this, they decided that they needed to make this idea of the East, there needed to be this concept of the East. The other, the nefarious, the sneaky, the mysterious, the strange and so they came up with this idea of making the East being basically Asia and and then going from there. Now the Romans had this a little bit and the Greeks had this a little bit so it wasn't that the English made it up completely from their own minds. For the Greeks, it was the Persians, for the Romans it was still the Persians and so the English kind of had oh yeah! this worked really well for the Greeks and the Romans we want to have this for ourselves so what they did was they named the far end of Asia, the Far East. They took the southern middle part of Asia and they called it the Middle East and then they took the Western end of Asia and they called it the near East because it was near Europe. In other words, what we call the Middle East was the near East what we call South Asia, was the the Middle East the near East is what we call the Middle East today, where we call South Asia today was the Middle East but then the Cold War started and we Americans went, huh! we can keep this East-West thing going but now we need the Russians to be the East because the East is evil and dangerous and exotic strange. so we'll make the Russians the new near East and we'll do the Eastern Bloc States as the new near East but if that's the near East the then the Middle East can't be the near East anymore so we renamed the near East the Middle East but then we needed a new name for the old Middle East so we named it South Asia. In our new naming scheme the Eastern Bloc States and the Soviet Union it never caught. Nobody started calling that the near East but they did call it the East and the Eastern Bloc in other words it partially worked it worked well enough it got what they wanted and now in a fact what they had done was they had successfully divorced East Germany from Western civilization in the minds of people but this isn't the first time that they divorced that somebody has divorced Western Civilization from the minds of people we had already done it to Egypt and Iraq. I just got through showing you that the West was founded in Egypt and Iraq and yet somehow we believe it's not in the West in fact even middle easterners will say it's not in the West. It's part of everybody's understanding of the world now and this is of course at the heart of Orientalism because the goal is to make it seem that the East is irrational, it's inefficient, it's authoritarian, and the West is democratic and liberated and everybody's happy it's all about ice cream. We build it into everything so I don't know if you've ever watched The Man in the high tower it's probably not worth watching uh the first season was really really amazing but then after that it kind of falls apart a little bit and you could tell they just didn't know where to go but it's about what would have happened if Japan and Germany had won World War II and so it's really weird watching Americans walking around in SS uniforms, you know Goose stepping around. So, the first season the whole time you keep thinking oh this is horrific well, not to ruin the story at any point for you in case you haven't seen it but at one point there is a good Japanese, that's a fun Trope. Good Japanese, bad Japanese uh right? we do this all the time good good Native American, bad

Native American yeah that's how we count though, it's Downtown Abbey everybody upstairs is wonderful some of the people downstairs are wonderful but some of the people downstairs are not wonderful, because we all know there are good Lower Class People yeah they're scum lower class people but upper class people are all wonderful because the guy who wrote Downtown Abbey, of course is a member of the nobility and so it's a giant propaganda piece, uh just just remember also he villainizes gay people which is interesting and Americans like this show so much. okay so, there's this good Japanese guy and he's trying to figure out the mess that they're in, because the Japanese are controlling California and they can barely hold on to it. Things are falling apart and they know that the Nazis are coming for them because of course that why would you make it ever anything with the Nazis they're eventually going to come for you? they went for each other. The Nazis spent a huge chunk of their time killing each other trying to move up in rank so this Japanese guy, there's a scene where he figures out what would have happened if Japan and Germany hadn't conquered the United States and what he sees is children licking ice cream and I thought really that's what you went to? that was the big moment, the big breakthrough moment there's balloons and there's children licking ice cream that's the difference ,that's the quantitative that was the qualitative difference that you saw between Nazism and what we have, surely there's something more.

Chapter 4

Identity is essential

I need to get into the conversation of identity because a part of all of this is identity so a few years ago I had a conversation with a Christian Egyptian woman, a Coptic woman and she said I'm an easterner and we in the east, and I was like wow here we go…

she's saying I'm an easterner she's embraced this idea, so now we need to get into identity we do something really interesting with identity identity is complicated and that's part of this problem because it's nested in the concept of Western Civilization so in other words when I talk about Western Civilization, I can't help but also then talk about identity because it plays such a massive role in The Way We shape our conversations, the way we understand who we are as individuals but also what we understand other people to be, because this is part of the authorizing process.

 so this identity conversation, I want to I want to bring up something interesting and it'll seem weird because it but I but it but when you think about it it's the right thing to do especially since I brought up the Irish earlier just to be clear I'm not I didn't like that book "How the Irish save civilization"
I love the Irish, so when the English start the next round of the troubles when they pull our Northern Ireland out of the EU and the Irish go now and stuff starts getting blown up and people start getting shot again because the English are idiots and they brexited, I'm going to be on Ireland's side. I'm outing myself right now when we talk about American presidents, you will hear people say Kennedy is the first Irish president, that's an interesting statement because it's a loaded statement he probably isn't and the reason I'm saying that is we we've had 46 presidents and 23 of them had Irish ancestry including Andrew Jackson and James K Polk and U.S Grant. Now. I don't think three men walked around going, I am irish-american but then when you say Kennedy's the first Irish president, it's kind of weird because what are you saying that because they didn't identify as Irish first they're not Irish? and what we really mean is Kennedy was the first Catholic President, right? you see see what I'm saying? like

for example if I told you Reagan was Irish does that come as a surprise if you're my age? it probably doesn't because there was conversation about Reagan being Irish in the 80s because the Speaker of the House Tip O'Neill was also Irish and so there was this weird thing where there was this Catholic Irish Speaker of the House in this Protestant Irish president and they're hanging out in France and they were friends. One was a Democrat, one was a republican but they liked each other and they got bills passed. They worked together, so there was that conversation but since then I doubt very much there's been much of a conversation, in fact Biden is Irish, he's not only Irish but United States after a few Generations nobody is only one thing anyway, you could try but yeah, y'all ain't gonna succeed. Your children, your grandchildren, your great-grandchildren somebody is going to start mixed reading. Yeah, this I promise you so we don't run around talking about Biden's Irishness, we still don't stop talking about Kennedy's Irishness. In fact, Biden is the second Catholic President, the majority of Americans know this, I think it's 60 percent but it's not an important conversation and because we're in a different place, right? the identity stuff has shifted a little bit, the way the identity thing gets to Biden is his religiosity when Democrats are asked how religious is he, by the way the majority of

Republicans know he's a Catholic. 55% of Republicans say yes Biden is a Cath; but when when people are asked, is Biden religious? 90% of Democrats say yes! he's at least a little religious, 45% of Republicans say yes! in other words, the way we stick identity on people has everything to do with the identity we hold for ourselves.

I mean I guess we could ask Biden, it never occurred to anybody to ask Biden I guess, because he would think he'd be the expert, like the fact that we have to survey Americans and they all have an opinion that's also fascinating to me like how does everybody have an opinion. Did you look it up? how did you know what Biden's religiosity is? how did you figure this out, like this mystery? my point is that when we think of how people we stick an identity marker on them and the identity markers can be really complicated because they can involve nationality, they can involve religion, they can involve race right? and those identity markers that were important at one point might be not important later on and so in the midst when we have a conversation about western civilization and the west and then how we think of ourselves that's what this is also about and usually when we say the West, we think of Athens and Rome and England and maybe even Germany and France reluctantly Spain and even though we think of Rome we're probably a little iffy about Italy which is another contradiction in this thing right? so let me give you an example what I mean by this, so when I was taught the part where they talk about the steam engine, I'm probably remembering this incorrectly but I swear at one point probably third grade I have it in my head and I'm probably wrong, I was taught that Robert Fulton invented the steam engine, now the funny thing about that of course is the steam engine was like a century old at that point so it'd be really hard for him to have invented the steam engine but it's the same type of story that we did with everything right? Ben Franklin invented the glasses it's not true he didn't invented the glasses. That Henry Ford invented the car again not true, even the stuff that you think is true is probably wrong it looks like an Australian family did flight before the Wright brothers and an English guy definitely did the light bulb before editing in other words everything we were taught was wrong at that level but okay, so then later on in my life as by the time I'm in college, I was taught that the steam engine was invented by Thomas Savory and Thomas newcomen, Savory did the first one and then newcomen did the next one and so you know you needed to mention both of them. Cool ! that's interesting, but it's not true. There was an Italian, before Thomas Savory, a guy named Giovanni branca who did a steam engine before him.

in fact there was a guy before him a Spaniard his name was Geronimo, they are Allianz II Beaumont, well I think that's his name. He invented the steam engine like 200 years before Robert Fulton stuck one in a boat, a hundred years before Thomas Savory and Thomas newcombin and honestly that's not the start of the steam engine either, there was a Turk named takiyadin who invented the steam engine in the year 1551, 60 years before the Spaniard did it in the Ottoman Empire in fact that's still not the birth of the steam engine.

 The steam engine was made by a guy named Heron, Heron was in the Library of Alexandria in Egypt and he made the steam engine 1500 years before takiyadin. We have had the steam engine for two thousand years now.

Now, when I mentioned Heron I didn't say it, I almost said it but I caught myself, I almost said he was a Greek from Alexandria Egypt at The Great Library and invented the steam engine the reason I caught myself, is because of the identity thing which I'm gonna I'm not done talking about but before I move away from Heron, I just want to point out what he did, he made two steam engines in fact one of them was actually a static rocket and it just spun. So he didn't just invent the steam engine, he also invented the world's first ever rocket. It didn't go anywhere but it was a rocket, the other thing he did, was he made a mechanical play with gears, I was also taught that the gear was invented like 300 years ago but he 2 000 years ago made a play that actually had gears in it, in fact we now have a thing called the anti-cathedral device. The anticothelial device was found off the coast of anticipira, is a metal box for the longest time archaeologists had no idea what to do with it, somebody went what if we x-rayed it and they did it, they x-rayed it.

It has gears in it the thing is 2000 years old and then they figured out what it was. Well, recently we finally figured out what this thing was. It was a computer, it was an analog computer, a mechanical computer not a digital computer, it wasn't electronic, it had gears in it and what you would do is you would enter the date on the top and then it would rotate the constellations into place, so it was an astronomical device computer so you could know what constellations you would see that night, think about how complicated it would have been to put that kind of data into the form of gears and then stick it into a box and make it work. Where you're putting something as complicated as a date into it by rotating the gears, this is not nothing. So Heron had this thing with gears in it, with levers by the way with bells and whistles on it, you would turn it on and then you would go sit down and watch and what the gears would do is, it would cause the scenes to shift and you could have an object move across for example you could have waves and then a boat and then you could have sound effects with the the Bell and the whistle and the clacking and then the scene could shift because you had all these different things that would move into place and you could have a scene where a boat goes across the water and lands on the shore and a hero moves out. In other words, he invented a TV, It was just a mechanical TV. 2 000 years ago, is that crazy? now I said already I almost admitted to you as Greek.

let me tell you what why I'm telling you this so my uh my family from my father's mother so my grandmother's family a Swede from Finland, so I was raised to believe I was a swede, because swedes are cool and I was raised to be racist against Finns. is it racist, are Finns a race, anti-nationalists against Finns. There because Finns are a nation not a race so in other words, I was taught Finn and swedes are wonderful. Now, here's the weird thing about Finland svenskard is there's swedes from Finland and the reason there were swedes in Finland is Sweden conquered Finland. so they were the Nobles who went into rule Finnish land and pesantize the Fins, so they were not good guys and they ruled over Finland in this really nasty way for centuries and then in the Napoleonic Wars Sweden picked the wrong side and they sided with the French. The French lost, Napoleon

Was Defeated and so as part of Sweden's punishment Russia took Finland from it. The Russians then went to the swedes living in Finland and they said hey! you guys know how to control these fins and rule them you already have your little fiefdom set up with Barons and dukes and counts and stuff, you keep doing that but in our name and we'll leave you where you are and you just pay us taxes and the Finland Spence car went yeah! it's a good deal so basically we lost nothing losing to you in the war and they're like yeah ! sure that's how you want to feel about it. In other words, the Finland Spence car are not the most popular people in Finland. They're about six percent of the population and they're you know, it's an ugly history. Until World War II and then we made up for it uh the swedes fought side by side with the fins against the Russians and All Is Forgiven and the Fins and the swedes are like the bopsy twins of Europe now. I don't know if you caught this in the news or a few months ago but the prime minister of Finland said we want to join NATO but we can't unless the swedes join and it's because Finland will never do anything without Sweden and Sweden will never do anything out without Finland and Sweden said we've been holding on our neutrality for a long time but, if you need to join NATO and we think you do because the Russians are a real threat we have to join

NATO to support you like that's how their relationship is, they're very cute they should totally just get married and get it over, they're already married so in other words, if I went to Finland even though there might be some latent resentment left. I'm probably okay I'm not like scared or anything about it. I haven't spent years now trying to overcome my anti-Finnish and embrace the fact that I'm more Finnish than Swedish. So she had a Swedish name, she spoke Swedish, she identified as Swedish, it's just genetically she was mostly Finnish see how complicated this guy all of a sudden but now here's the really weird twist and it's why I'm bringing this up if you're a six percent minority in a place and you only want to breed with your own Nation, it's going to get cousiny really fast you know what I mean? you're probably doing your children and grandchildren a huge disservice at some point you're going to want to open up to the possibility of marrying into one of the locals and that's what my ancestors did. So what I am is I'm paternally Swedish and I had a Swedish male ancestor who married a Finn and then maybe he married a Swede that child married a Swede but then there were like two more Fins and that and then a Swede again in other words as time went by, we effectively became genetically Finnish because that Swedish DNA just kept shrinking every time there was a marriage to a local, and that's what happened to Heron when the Greeks conquered Egypt 300 years before Heron's birth, the Greeks definitely separated themselves out from the Egyptians because they saw the Egyptians as inferior. But after 15 Generations, there was no way Heron wasn't part Egyptian. In other words calling Heron the Greek scientists from Egypt is really an interesting proposition, because how Greek was he? how Egyptian was he? after 15 Generations in Egypt? how Greek were the Greeks? if nothing else their culture was modified by the Egyptians they lived around their DNA was modified because you know they were marrying into them, not Cleopatra. But when I say when I said Cleopatra, you went oh! the Egyptian pharaoh, the woman, Cleopatra by the way it's the seventh I'm keeping track. Cleopatra the seventh is the famous One. Cleopatra the seventh, that you identify as Egyptian with zero percent Egyptian, so it her family tree is wonky and difficult, because on two occasions she had an uncle Mary and niece so I don't know how to do this because I can't count the generations back because what am I supposed to do with Denise Uncle thing. Twice, so there's two ways to count it right? You count seven generations because you count the niece as a separate generation or five generations and you make your life not a nightmare. So I'm doing five, if you go back five generations the way to do this is, the math on this, the math is fun and the really cool thing. You take two to the power of the generation you're trying to go to, so you're zero Generations away from you, two to the zero power is one, your parents are one generation away from you two to the first power is two your grandparents are two away from you so two squared is four your great grandparents are two cubed that's eight by the time you go five generations back so three greats and then grandparents you end up with 32 ancestors, you should have 32 great, great, grandparents, she had four a Persian and three Greeks it's actually worse if you go one generation forward you go to the fourth generation she only had two and then when she got to the two that two, had three kids one of the kids married his niece, his niece was the product of his brother and sister. So I don't even know where to go other than oh my God! but notice what we do, we go Cleopatra the Egyptian, Heron the Greek. Heron was definitely very Egyptian by the time we got to the First Century A.D. Cleopatra was definitely very non-Egyptian at all in any way shape or form because she had been so secluded from Egyptian culture because the Greeks looked down on the Egyptians so intensely that they went out of their way to inbreed to try to prevent Egyptian DNA from entering the Royal Family. It's intense, let me give you another example what I mean by this the guy who invented philosophy, some people call him Thales, Americans usually say Thales. So I'm just going to say Thales to make our lives easy.

Thales the Greek philosopher who invented philosophy, wasn't Greek, Isn't that cool? the guy who invented Greek philosophy wasn't Greek he lived in a Greek city the city was called Miletus. Miletus is today in Turkey, he spoke Greek but he also spoke Phoenician because his family was from Lebanon they were Phoenicians, they had moved to miletus for business purposes he grew up in miletus and then produced the world's first ever work of philosophy a book titled **Water Is Best,** a Phoenician invented philosophy in a Greek city in what is today turkey but when we think of Thales, we think of a Greek, when we think of Heron, we think of a Greek, when we think of Cleopatra, we think of an Egyptian. that's what I mean. What we do is we have this tendency to be selective with how we apply the identities and that gets all sorts of messy. Okay, so now let's do this let's shift now that I've got you thinking about identity and how we're careless with it.

Chapter 5

Criteria for being West

Now I want to found western Civilization. so what is it that makes something West and something not West, so this is part of the reason why my title was meant to bring out contradictions. The East-West Paradigm at some level is nonsensical because it assumes that there isn't connectivity and can with the other side and cultural sharing, so at some level there is no Western Civilization, that's a construct that's part of our imagination. At another level there is a western civilization because there is a geographical region that had a lot more connection with other place than with other places one way to think of this then would be if you made the Indus River the boundary for Western Civilization everything to the west of the Indus is Western Civilization, but that doesn't mean everything to the east of the Indus is into civilization or is it Eastern civilization because if nothing else Indian civilization is so different from Korean or Japanese civilization right? it's Preposterous actually to start lumping together about everything west of the Indus does have strong connectivity and here's why, it's the Mediterranean when we think of bodies of water, we usually think of them as dividers that's because of our bias the Pacific and the Atlantic are dividers because they're so big they really do divide the old world from the new world but the Mediterranean isn't a divider it's a connector it has the exact opposite role. It's just small enough of a body of water that getting across. It isn't too difficult, it's insulated enough that it does have tempests, which are the Mediterranean Cyclones, but they're never as intense as hurricanes, the ancient world you just didn't sail during the Tempest season which was basically fall and winter you just stayed out of the Seas and yeah that way you can avoid it and so what ends up happening is the Mediterranean connects because it's a highway, it's way easier to move goods and people by boat than it is by land, land is a pain because you've got to build a road then you've got to maintain the road you've got to make wagons and the wheels are constantly breaking and you can hardly put anything in a wagon and then you have all these stupid animals, you have to feed right and they get oh! they need water or they'll die right? so if you're trying to get from Egypt to Morocco don't go by land, go by sea. You'll get there really fast. It'll be very efficient and your life will be relatively easy. So what ends up happening then is all the civilizations near and around the Mediterranean end up intimately connected together so if we if we accept that premise then yeah! there is some regionalism to it even though at some level, it's still a little bit of an artificial device In other words, I'm admitting that we're maybe doing a little bit of a stretch here but let's do it anywhere for the sake of the exercise, Okay so we've accepted that it was born in Iraq and Egypt and then we've created a geographical boundary for now we can talk about the elements, so some of the elements of of Western Civilization tends to be that they were Western civilization was Pagan with pantheons, the Egyptian Pantheon, the Roman Pantheon, the Greek pantheon, the pantheon that went through the Fertile Crescent, but then there's this, other religion Judaism which was by the way henotheistic originally not monotheistic, so it wasn't that the Jews said there was only one God, monotheism says there's only one God, the Jews said there is only one God for us. Y'all have a different God that's henotheism. It's an important distinction, it's not to say that there isn't some monotheism in Judaism today, I'm talking about ancient Judaism they were henotheistic. A lot of Jews are still henotheistic today. So in other words there was this henotheistic religion that then spawned off Christianity and then later on Islam, so two religions came off of this one religion and that's what we tend to think of as a western trait. Christianity not the other two not Judaism and Islam so much but definitely Christianity although maybe Judaism is a little bit better accepted today but not for the bulk of European history right? European histories Pogrom after pogrom, after pogrom, after pogrom, until we get to the pogrom of pogroms, the Holocaust and then, Europeans go okay I guess we should stop killing them, but it's like this reluctant almost I've I miss it. So if we accept that that's the religious background for this, then there's the birth of government in Egypt, there's a birth of writing and Sumer, what are the other elements? one place you can look to is the 18th dynasty of Egypt. The 18th dynasty of Egypt did something really remarkable, one of the things it did was it actually started an Empire Egypt built the world's first Empire that stretched from one country to the next, the 18th Dynasty conquered part of Libya. They conquered Veronica, Eastern Libya. They conquered the northern part of the Sudan, they went into Palestine, they went all the way into Syria and they created an Empire. Well, imperialism is the history of Western Civilization, so there's that element, that's interesting the 18th Dynasty also invented a convenience industry. So for example, you could write down on a stone (they like to use Limestone slabs) you could write down on a slab, your laundry list and send your laundry and they would wash it and then they would bring it to you or you could put a grocery list and you could call them up on the phone, either you would give the list to a boy and the boy would take it to the store he'd buy your groceries and bring them to you. There was this entire giant apparatus, built around convenience in the 18th Dynasty in Egypt. They took history to a new level, so by the end of the 18th Dynasty they did a better job of chronicling their events, so that by the 19th Dynasty they were doing a really good job of it. 18th Dynasty they were still figuring this out so they would for example there was an amazing photo oh! because as a warrior, he would lead his man into battle from the front line and he was a general and he commanded his men and he never lost the battle and we know that he was in 17 military campaigns because it chronicled all that. By the way, there were prolific writers, they wrote poetry they wrote Love Letters, they kept track of who lived there, so they did a census, there is a little town in Upper Egypt, if you go there, we know more about the people living in that town over the course of a 400 years span of time, because we have their notes, we have their love letters, we have the Poetry they're writing each other, we have their laundry lists, and we have their grocery lists, we know intimate details about where each person lived and What kind of Life they lived. We know more about them from 3500 years ago, than we know about Americans from 200 years ago. In other words that's a hint of the kind of hyper chronicling that you all do now on social media, what did you eat today, all I got to do is look at your social media account I will know how's your dog doing, you've told me that too. what's the latest choreographed picture of the idyllic life you're leading, where you were careful not to show the the factory in front of your front door by taking the picture in an angle, so that all we saw was the sky and the trees. It's all there. Make sure not to give anybody your address because they can Google Map it and they'll see the factory, you know! carefully choreographed. Fast forward make it 6th Century BC there's a guy named Cyrus the Great, Persian, in fact he's the guy who creates the Persian Empire. When he does it, he issues the world's first ever Bill of Rights, when I say Bill of Rights you think Western Civilization, there it is. The Persians they beat everybody to it, by the way just for the record that Bill of Rights that's almost 2600 years old. it's over 2500 years old. Almost 26 centuries, Ban slavery human sacrifice and it guaranteed freedom of religion, in fact it encouraged Freedom religion. The Persians told everybody in the Empire, if your temples are in disrepair, we will fix it for you using Government funding, so after the Neo-Babylonian Empire,they conquer the Jews in Palestine and dragged some of those Jews to Babylon not to be slaves but to live in Babylon. They were forcibly relocated to Babylon when when kurosh conquered Babylon, he told the Jews no you can live anywhere you want, we're not doing that anymore. There's no slavery in my Empire, there's no forced living anywhere in my Empire, and so a bunch of them wanted to go back to Palestine, the Temple of Solomon had been destroyed by the Neo-Babylonians because they hated the Jews and they just wanted to hurt them so they tore down the Temple of Solomon and when they read the Bill of Rights, they go hey! can we get a new Temple of Solomon? Kurosh is like yes! of course everybody gets their temples rebuilt and he said okay yeah! show me the plans, let's just say they added stuff from the original Temple, for example they built a giant human-made Mesa, and then put the second temple of Solomon on top, and so kurosh is looking at it and he goes wait, what? that's like a mountain, a flat mountain, the Babylonians tore that down? I don't even know how anybody built it, let alone tore it down, and you guys are like yeah they really hated us and so kurosh goes well I we're gonna do it. We promised you, we'd to do it. We're gonna build it but I only know one people on Earth that can build mountains, it'll be Persian gold but it's going to be Egyptian engineers, and they went and grabbed Egyptian engineers and they built the temple mount with Persian gold, and that's why Kurosh, is in the Bible.

Thales shortly afterwards, a few decades later invents philosophy miletus. It spreads, it goes to Athens, the Athenians fall in love with it. A woman, teaches Socrates. Well, I got left out of your stories didn't it? Socrates's teacher was a woman named Aspasia. The reason why that I got left out of your history is because Once we became Christian, we didn't like the idea that women were teachers and leaders and so there was a systematic attempt to delete all the women leaders and all the women philosophers from the history textbooks.

Chapter 6

The Great Library

So if you look up Aspasia, you will find people saying yeah she may not have been real, why would Socrates tell us that a mythical person taught him philosophy what's the point in even making up the story, what's the likelihood that she wasn't Real. It's preposterous, but it fits our patriarchal orientation. The Persians and the Greeks are in this epic back and forth and eventually the Persians get bored with the Greeks and stop fighting them and then Alexander the Great conquers them out of the blue and this is this unbelievable event and then that Greek civilization starts to come apart and gets replaced by this Roman civilization and the Romans are amazing conquerors, they take the Greek Phalanx they they upgrade it they turn it in the Roman legion the Persians eventually recover from the great conquest and now the new Clash is between the Persians and the Romans, and it'll last 53 BC when the Battle of Karach until the rise of

Islam when it ends. So the Muslims start conquering Persian in 633. So, 53 BC to 633 almost seven centuries, the Persians and the Romans fight it out, brutal nasty knocked down ,drag out fights, but in the middle of all of this there's one thing that's really powerful and important for our purposes and it's The **Great Library**, one of the Greeks who went with Alexander and conquered the Persians, his name was Ptolemy, the first so tear Ptolemy the Savior, that's the title he took. He goes and carves Egypt out of this Greek Empire when Alexander the Great dies, because he thought Egypt was the best piece of real estate in Alexander's Empire. And then he founds The Great Library, the idea behind the great libraries it'll be the world's repository for information and what they're going to do is they're going to bring books from every society and every culture there and keep a copy and they're going to invent things. The first thing on Earth called a museum was one of the buildings at The Great Library, it was a museum for all the latest Advanced Tech. There was no such thing as copyright, the idea was that you could go to Alexandria, visit the library, see the museum, see the advanced Tech and then build on it but then once you built on it, you were supposed to bring your advances there, so that the next generation of advances could be made based on yours. That was the idea behind the museum not so you could stick art and ancient relics in it. It was supposed to be so that the world could Advance technologically at its height, The Great Library may have reached as many as a million books, I actually think a million is probably the right number, I've seen two million feel like that's too many. I've seen 200 000 I feel like that's too few. To give you an idea what a million books is, the Library of Congress, the United States Library of Congress reached the million bookmark in 1905. so in terms of quantity of information, The Great Library was on far with where we were in 1905. Quality no, but quantity yes, because right by 1905 we had flights, the light bulb and steam trains.

But remember Heron, he was at The Great Library so they had steam they just hadn't made trains yet. If they had had a little bit more time they might have but they run out of time. They run out of time because Rome converts to Christianity. Now, this isn't me abashing Christianity, I'm not in the mood to bash anybody. I just want to tell you the story because it's important that we acknowledge what happened as Rome switched to being Christian and dumped its pagan Roots. It also started to slowly move away from this idea that it needed to be Advanced technologically, and in 391 A.D it took that to the maximum level when Emperor Theodosius issued a decree declaring that the Roman Empire was not it wasn't just that Christianity was the official religion, it wasn't just that Christianity was the state's religion, it was also the only religion. Non-Christians were no longer welcome in the Empire Jews and pagans needed to convert or leave and when that happened, the Archbishop of Alexandria, Archbishop Theophilus, issued his own decree asking the Christian population of Alexandria to go ahead and get rid of the pagans and the Jews. They went to the Jewish quarter, Alexandria was the largest Jewish City on the planet. So the second Greek Ptolemy Philadephus had such a Jewish large Jewish population in Alexandria, that couldn't speak Hebrew, so they didn't know how to read their holy texts, that he decided to commission a Greek translation of the Old Testament into Greek so that the Greek-speaking Jews living in Alexandria would be able to access their holy texts. So he he got 70-something rabbis, we don't know the exact number and he made the septijuent which means 70. and the septijuent was because he had 70 rabbis translate the Old Testament so that it could weed out bias and error and they would merge the 70 translations into one so they could get an accurate translation. We have since, we see found the the Dead Sea Scrolls which are which were older but not by much I think they were two or three hundred years old so now we have the original Old Testament material in the original Hebrew and we've compared them you don't need to change your translations it septet you into spot on. It was an amazing translation in other words he pulled it off.

The mob goes to the Jewish Corridor and just Begins massacring the Jews, when they're done destroying the Jewish quarter, which won't be inhabited again for another another 1500 years, they then go and try to find the pagans. The problem with the pagans is they were intermingled with the Christians so you just literally had to knock on doors and go you Pagan pretty much everybody is going to deny it, so then you go who are your Pagan neighbors? and then right now you can find out because right, people will rat each other out, it's hilarious.

They then go to The Great Library. The Great Library was run by a woman named Hypatia. Hypatia was wasn't actually technically a pagan, she was a theist, so she did believe that there was an entity that created the universe. A single entity but she didn't think that anybody could know its nature, so she rejected Christianity and but the majority of the students at The Great Library, the majority of the professors of The Great Library were in fact pagan. And so the mob decides to get rid of The Great Library and they destroy it. But we as a society Get Lucky, because before they destroyed it by a few decades there was a Persian Emperor who got jealous of

The Great Library his name was Shahpur. Shahpur wanted his own Great Library, he defeats a Roman Emperor. Valerian, he captures two intact Roman Legions, he sells one into slavery in China, takes the money from the sale and then he uses that money and orders the Roman Legions to build him two brand new cities one of them is Gandhi Shahpur, in Gandhi Shahpur, he builds an academy that will be the Persian equivalent to The Great Library and he starts collecting books he's having trouble getting Roman books because the Romans and the Persians hate each other so much but he has he's having no trouble getting Chinese texts and Indian texts and so he's adding those to the Persian knowledge. He gets Lao Tzu books, one of the greatest philosophers in human history, 600 years earlier but he gets his books which is amazing because when Chin the Great unifies India he bans Lao Tzu and starts wiping out Lao's works but now there's a place for them to survive. When the Great Library is burnt, a group of Romans decide to recover and they do it at the Academy. The Academy of Athens, when they do this at the Academy of Athens, that gets banned. So they get some of the books together at the Academy but Emperor Justinian goes nah we got rid of the Great Library we don't need an academy to replace it those Greek scholars, In 529 when the academy is banned grab all their books they jump on a ship they head to Syria, they cross Syria they get to what would roughly be the Iraq-Syria border today it was roughly where the Roman-Persian border was, and they they approach the Persians and they say we want Asylum and the persons go yeah of course who would want to live under a Roman rule anyway these guys are crazy and they go yeah not for us only we want Asylum for our books and the Persians go to your books and they go yeah we're we're bringing everything we have left that hasn't been burnt by Christian mobs and the Persians go oh come with us and they take them to Gandhi Shahpur and they take all those books and they merge them in. Emperor khusrl, is the guy who does this. So now, at Gandhi Shahpur they have all these Roman and Greek and Egyptian works and they're sitting there with all these Chinese and Persian and Indian works, and it kind of recovered the loss of The Great Library a little bit. Rome and Persia keep fighting, they do one giant slug Fest in the early 600s, nasty brutal Affair. The Persians capture turkey, Syria, Palestine, Egypt. It looks like Rome is going to go down in a ball of flames, but the Romans somehow where, get out of it in fact because one of the Persian generals decides to Rebel, he takes the chunk of Rome that he captured (and) he creates a third Little Empire. Eventually he invades Persia, overthrows the Persian Emperor, (he) becomes the new Persian Emperor and is stabbed to death a few days later.

Chapter 7

The Manifestation of Islam

The Romans are like wow, because military was touching go there for a while and then something amazing happens.

There's a new religion and it's Islam. The prophet Muhammad dies in 632. That year, the Khalifa, his follower the first ruler after the prophet orders that the Arabian Peninsula be conquered; and unified for the first time in Arab history the Arabian Peninsula was ruled by a single state within a year, that same year 633 Abubakar (the successor of the Prophet Muhammad, Peace and Blessings of Almighty Allah be Upon him) launches two armies at the same time simultaneously, one into the Persian Empire, one into the Roman Empire. Outnumbered, out manned, out technology there's no way the Arabs should Prevail within a few decades they completely conquer the Persian Empire, it was 1200 years old at that point.

Can you imagine a 1200 year old Empire? you can't comprehend it not being there. They bring the Romans to their knees, they don't finish them off. But by the time they're gone, so from 633 the moment they start the Conquering to 711, the moment they've conquered Spain, they owned everything from Pakistan to Spain and Central Asia they built the largest Empire in human history, in just a few decades sixty percent of the world's Christian population, the Empire itself is two percent Muslim but it owns sixty percent of the world's Christians. It was an Empire of Buddhists and Hindus there were even some pagans hanging around and Zoroastrians.

The Arabs were a strange conqueror population, because they weren't forcibly converting people by the sword, they weren't Mass genociding whole populations, they weren't enslaving one-third of Gaul, they did fight in France just for the record. The Battle of tour, also known as a battle of Poitier against Charles Mattel and the French win just for the record but the Arabs as they were retreating carved off narbone and continue to rule a piece of France for a few centuries. These Arabs were actually shot or humble so when they conquered Persia, they went to the Persians and they went dude, we don't know how to run an Empire. We just started ruling ourselves, we don't know what we're doing here, you guys are amazing at this, what we need you to do is keep running the empire, we don't even know how to mint coins, the first Arab coins show three men standing next to each other, they're holding a cross in one hand and a globe with a cross sticking out of it. So, they got a cross in both hands because they took the Roman mint and they just began counterfeiting Roman coins. in fact the word **"Flus"** which is the word for money (in Arabic) comes from the Roman **"Follus"** which was one of the coins that they were counterfeiting, those Arabs walked into Gandhi Shakur, after conquering it, and they turned to the Persians and they went what's that ? and the Persians go (they said), it's an academy. The Arabs go cool, what is that? because the repository of all the knowledge of the world that we know of, and the Arabs go(they said) show us, and the Persians go(said) what choice do we have? take them in.

The Arabs go (said) teach us, and the pressures go what choice do we have? we will (teach you). It takes a while, it doesn't happen right away but in the 8th Century, AL-kindi begins converting these texts from Greek to Arabic and that's a huge leap because now it means a larger portion of the population can start to read them.

A guy named Al Khwarizmi, a Muslim Persian in the Arab Empire decides to start focusing heavily on Hindu mathematics. Al Khwarizmi invents algebra and Arabic numerals. So, the next time you're doing math, remember to thank Al Khwarizmi that you're not using an Abacus to do Roman numerals, which are impossible. Really try, set up normal Roman numerals put a minus sign under and try and subtract Roman numerals from Roman numerals, you'll tear your hair out. Forget multiplication and division, Al Khwarizmi creates a math system that you can work on. He's so Advanced, he invents algorithms 1200 years ago. In fact algorithm was the Roman attempt to say his name Al Khwarizmi. so every time you say algorithm, you're actually saying this Persian philosopher's name.

Around the year 800 the Arabs invented modern agriculture the way they did that was they DE-pesentized the population of farmers that they had inherited when they conquered the Persian and Roman Empires, and they created private property with the hope that then the Persians who were now free, who now owned their own land could do whatever they wanted to with it. They would experiment and they'd figure out the best ways to do agriculture instead of just doing the same old thing over and over again. In other words, the incentive of profit motivation might trigger something and it does, one of the things that they figure out is crop rotation. They're the guys who invent that, they also realize don't keep planting the same crop over and over again what if there's a blight? what if there's an insect plague? you're reliant on one food makes you dangerously at the mercy of that food, and so you need to have Diversified crops so one of the things the Arabs did was they went around looking for new things to grow, and they're the guys who start the coffee Industry. They take these beans that they find in Ethiopia that they realize they can do something with and they bring them to Yemen and they plant them in the province of Yemen named Mocha, and start the coffee industry. They also realize you can pack fresh food on a ship and send it to the other side of Asia, all you had to do is pack it full of ice and so they were sending fresh food to China and India by packing ships full of ice. They had Plumbing and by Plumbing, I mean fresh water was pumped in, sewage water was pumped out. They invented water wheels to make the pumping work, so you could just use the power of a river to run your pump, they lit up their streets at night. So, in other words if you walk down the streets of Baghdad a thousand years ago, as you're walking down that street at night there were oil lamps. In other words if I took a satellite and I put it in orbit around the Earth, a thousand years ago and I stuck it. So, it was always at night so I'd see the whole planet at night photographed. The whole planet's pitch dark except for everything from Iraq to Pakistan, the cities twinkled like they do now. Ibnul Haitham speculated that all objects in the universe exerted gravity, I don't know how you observe that. I mean I get that the floor is exerting gravity over me? but he said all objects, how's the wall pulling me? I don't experience that. He also said light has a finite speed and it travels in waves, his book of Optics was 1021, they dabbled in psychology, Ibn Kaldun comes along, says it's okay to read history but you need to be a skeptic, historians lie, don't believe everything you read. Don't read Herodotus and take him at his word because he's a liar, we need to think about what he's saying and ask why is he saying. what he's saying? he also says we should have a systematic study of politics and sociology and demographics. In other words, he's the inventor of the social sciences including their little separate categories, In other words he's the founder of political science. Maimonides is a Jewish Arab from Spain, he'll laments the death of Hebrew, so Hebrew died harder than Latin died. When Hebrew died, they lost a lot of vocabulary and they lost the grammar system. They kind of vaguely knew what the grammar system ought to look like because they had holy texts but it wasn't enough, it wasn't enough to reconstruct the language, it wasn't enough to learn it and speak it. So here's what Maimonides did, he realized that

Hebrew and Arabic were very close cousins, maybe brother and sister actually. So he took Arabic grammar, he studied it until he understood it. He took the Hebrew vocabulary that they had from the holy text, he plugged it in and then whenever he was missing a word, he just grabbed the Arabic word and stuck it in and he brought Hebrew back which is unbelievable. Name another language that was resurrected from death. I don't know one, languages die that's it. They're finished, except for Hebrew; that's that time period. So notice the dates though we are told that the Dark Ages start when Rome falls on September 476 A.D I told you at the beginning Rome didn't fall that day, it fell May 29 1453. How do I know? on that date in September in 476 all that happened was Romulus Augustus the Western Roman Emperor took off his purple robes, stuck it in a box with a note sent it to Emperor Zeno, the Eastern Roman Emperor and said there's no reason for two Emperors, let's just do one. You're it, I abdicate that's not the same as Rome fell, on May 29 1453 Ottoman soldiers entered Constantinople the Roman capital and captured it and Rome ceased to own any real estate that's when a state Falls is when it doesn't own real estate. That's how I know Rome didn't fall that moment but what we are told is that the Dark Ages, the Middle Ages, the medieval period starts with the fall of Rome in 476 and doesn't end until sometime around 1492 that it lasts a thousand years. There's a thousand years without knowledge but I just showed you that there was actually extraordinary developments that were taking place, including calculus 600 years before Newton. Ibnul Haitham stated Newton's first law of motion 600 years before Newton, he he actually described Kepler's first law of planetary motion 500 years before Kepler. when I was working on my graduate degree, I started to get into Heidegger who is very controversial but that doesn't mean you throw the baby out with a bath water, he was a Nazi for 11 months, bad Heidegger, bad, he denounced the Nazi party after 11 months and said you're all a bunch of Charlatans, I reject you and then he spent the rest of World War II as an outcast but still that 11 months were gross. He got his Professor fired and then took his job, his Professor was that guy named Husserl, he was Jewish. I'm doing this because I just don't want anybody to be confused about why I'm reading Heidegger, I'm reading Heidegger and I realized something in his bibliography, he's quoting Ibnul Haitham and Ibn Sinai and at the time I didn't know who they were, so I went who are these guys? when he was quoting Ibn Sinai, the reason he was quoting him is because his teacher whose sorrow who by the way was brilliant he shouldn't have fired him. This is ugly, who sorrow had taken Hegel and Ibn

Cena and merged them and created a new branch of philosophy called phenomenology so when Heidegger was taking his thing on being in time to the next level, he was building off of that and then of course um that became the moment when philosophy in the world completely changed. Everybody who hates Heidegger is still a Heideggerian. There's No Going Back, Heidegger changed philosophy grabbed it he shook it, he flipped it upside down and he redid it but part of its inspiration for this was that conversation I had with you earlier about Ibn Cena (Ibn Sinai) and the nature of the universe, he took and built on that and then changed philosophy forever.

So even though the guy was a thousand-year-old thinker, he was still playing a major role a hundred years ago and changing the way we do philosophy, in other words there's no separation between any of this it's all connected together.

Chapter 8

Destruction of the Books

One last thing, so the Arabs had idiomatically translated Aristotle into Arabic, when the Spanish were conquering Spain from the Muslims they kept encountering libraries, the popes kept issuing edicts to burn all the books just like when they had burnt The Great Library and just when they shut down the Academy of Athens, they wanted to continue this. The thinking went, you only need one book, it's the Bible why are we doing the science stuff? we don't need this, what we need to do is Purge the libraries of all these books that make me feel uncomfortable oh no that's now, oh wait no that was then too. It's so confusing how? nothing changes, we don't learn. Well, the monks who were ordered to destroy the books, were the Benedictines and the Dominican monks. The Benedictines and the Dominican monks didn't obey the order, what they did was they dug giant underground libraries beneath their monasteries, when they would show up to the place with the Muslim library that they had to burn, they would read, they had a guy who would stand here and they had the book they would turn the book, so it was facing him so he could read it, he was a human card catalog, he knew the list the names of all the books they had in their secret underground Library. So as you would walk by he'd read it, if he recognized the book, he'd give you one signal and you'd dump it in a file in the middle of the town. If he didn't recognize it, he'd give you another signal and you'd walk over to a cart where they had a hidden panel and you'd Slide the book into that and then you'd walk back and you'd go grab another book and then he'd carry it. So that that guy could read it and oh that one goes in this file, and then afterwards they'd set that file on fire so they could show everybody they were burning the books, and then they'd sneak the other books into their underground Library where they were busy translating it from Arabic into ancient Greek and Latin and that's how we have Plato and Aristotle. We would have lost it all because the Christians were going around burning everything. What happened that was not only did the Benedictine and the Dominican monks have a second thoughts about this and refused to follow their orders, it's good to not follow orders sometimes but the Italians went you know what I miss the good old days when we had science and math and philosophy. Why don't we do that again? and sometime around 1300 they do the Renaissance. 1300, the Crusades end in 1291. After the Crusaders start coming back, they go you know what we saw when we were there murdering all those Muslims and Jews? they had indoor plumbing and Medicine and crop rotation. They're talking about things have gravity, and that light has a finite speed and that the Universe originates from a point of information, and the Italians go oh wow! that's so cool let's do that here.

Chapter 9

Questions & Answers

Al right let's do Q&A for a few minutes.

Okay so the question is, does the Arabs being in Sicily for two centuries have an impact on the creation of the Renaissance?

The answer is yeah; There was a guy named Frederick II. He happens to be one of my favorite ever rulers, so the Vikings conquer northern France at one point they renamed northern France after themselves. They were the north-men Nordmen, Norseman, they rename it after themselves. They were called the Normans, they call it Normandy, the Normans at some point get really bored. They're like dude I'm sick of watching peasants grow things, so they're saying it in French but with a viking accent right, because they stopped speaking German they started speaking French so just imagine, so get that going in your head but do it in

French, Je mappels ben ya.. that must have been horrific for French speakers to hear this.

One day, they're just like you know what dude?, let's go kill somebody. Now The original killing event, they went to Spain actually and they captured marabous which today is Zaragoza. It was a Muslim City, they capture it and they're like wow, this is awesome. so I need you to have in your head redhead and blonde head Vikings with long hair and braids and big beards right, they're just they're just you know they got an axe they're ready to hack people to death, they get there and they see the Arabs doing philosophy and Math and Science and they go this is so cool, they take off their Viking clothing, they start wearing Jallabiya (Arab dressing) and they walk around learning Arabic and they blend into Arab Society in Zaragoza in Spain. Well, word gets back to Normandy and the Normans are like man! we could do this on a larger scale, so a group of them get in a ship, they sail all the way around Spain to Sicily. They get to Sicily, they conquer it, and then there have this really interesting situation because there's all these Arabic speaking people living there, there are there are people who are speaking Italian living there, and they're Christian because they had converted, it didn't tone them down yet they get toned down later right, they're still a little sociopaths and then little by little they start to marry into German royalty, this is complicated and eventually there's a guy named Frederick II; if you look at coins from the time period in Sicily, one side is in Arabic the other side is in Latin.

Frederick II actually had a bureaucracy made up of Christians, Jews and Muslims and he learned Arabic he didn't just learn Arabic, he spoke Italian and German and French and like I think two other languages, the dude was just is that a polyglot, he was that guy! and he would read texts in the original Arabic and then sometimes he'd translate them in Latin, he even did his own science. He's so in love with the Muslim world that after throwing the Crusaders out, he was approached to see if he wanted the title of king of Jerusalem and he didn't send an Army in conquer it was just a symbolic gesture. He eventually will become the Holy Roman Emperor which means he also owned Italy and Germany and he's spreading his ideas, he got into Falcon raid, the quintessential Arab sport, like he's out there with Falcons reading original Arabic script; learning how to do this and it pissed off the popes. He got excommunicated twice, he led an army to Rome twice, he conquered it and captured the pope and cut his head off a couple of times and instituted new popes, a couple of times because all that sciency stuff that he was learning was apparently corrupting his soul but yeah it's the same time period it's that moment when Italy is rethinking maybe burning the books wasn't a great idea, so you have two ways of thinking about this you can pretend that Islam held on to Western civilization while western civilization was burning itself to the ground and then Western Civilization just reconstituted itself or you can realize the truth which is that the Arabs were Western Civilization all along, the Islam didn't necessarily save something that it wasn't, it saved itself. It just took it to a new level the Arabs weren't doing something that was alien to them, they were part of western civilization. They even had a western civilization religion because right? Islamism (an) Abrahamic religion so they had all these Western Civilization Traditions, when they conquered that part of Rome and Persia that was part of western civilization that had never stopped being Western Civilization. What happened is you were taught it, in an Islamophobic way, so all the Muslim parts were just simply deleted. And so now we think of this as an East-West divide and somehow the Muslims are on the on the east side of it, they're not.

That woman when she told me Egyptians are easterners, she's just flat-out wrong, this is part of Orientalism. It's an attempt to make you see the world as US versus THEM.

It's not; it's just not. In Texas for example, we do community property divorce, we got that from Mexico. Mexico is Catholic, it didn't have divorce, Mexico got it from Spain. Spain is Catholic, Spain didn't have divorce. When the Arabs ruled Spain, they got sick of all the deadbeat husbands who were divorcing their wives for younger models and then leaving the children to be raised by those divorced wives who no longer had a source of income so there are all these kids living in the streets, so what they did in Spain was they created a system where all the property generated from the moment of the marriage is start to the moment that the marriages and got split in half period end story, that's community property Law. So you know you'll hear this thing that conservatives will say, I'm worried about Sharia law. Well, then don't get divorced. Because that's Muslim law. The taco, when the Spanish conquered Mexico, they said make this; the thing they were saying to make was **Shawarma** because the Spanish were Arabs, they were just self-hating Arabs who rejected their Arabness, so they had flatbread food with meat in the middle and then vegetables and a sauce you put on it, that they would fold like this the Aztecs go, we don't have those ingredients. The Spanish girl you're our slaves, we're going to kill you! make it anyway. So the Mexicans went fine, and then they made a tortilla and they put meat on it and they did a salsa, because they needed the ingredients because they didn't have tahini and they were just stuck. So, the next time you're eating **taco** remember, that it's actually originally Arab food, it's just a Native American version of Arab food.

 Al pastor you're like ah that'll work. I'll eat pork, that way I don't have to actually eat Arab food because Arabs don't eat pork. About 150 years ago Arabs started to move to Mexico, those Arabs wanted to make Shawarma. They're like my God! tacos are basically just Shawarma, how did that happen? because they didn't know the original story. So, they're sitting there going aah I want to make the Shawarma with lamb, I need a fatty meat, there just isn't enough fatty meat and Park;

and saw the era of Mexicans if you've ever been to Mexico, and you've eaten a whole off the thing, it's the Shawarma thing but it's got pork on it, in other words, Al pastor is Arab food twice, we're all interconnected. There's no separating any of this out from anything, are languages like this? Zenith, Nader, algebra those are all Arabic words. Zero is an Arabic word, Apricot is an Arabic word, there's no winning if you really wanted to do this, because there's no separating us out from each other.

Okay so the question is, why did Christianity reject all that philosophy and you know, set everything on fire at the same time that Muslims were embracing it?

I don't think there's a simple answer. I think you know, there's a historical moment that Christians found themselves in, as the Roman Empire was in Decline, the Roman Empire almost went away in the third Century. Diocletian saved it and reconstituted it by that point it goes christian and then on as the Roman Empire goes christian, it's in a terrible position, it's economies garbage, the population is poor, the population is small. Rome at one point was a million and a half people.

 By the time we get to the sixth Century A.D there was about 50,000 Romans living in the city. Rome itself was diminished and I think in that moment, there was this sense of it's hopeless everything is falling apart around us, let's turn to religion. We'll focus on religion, we'll just try to save our souls, we're not going to worry about the material world, and so I think that was the basis of the rejection that it came out of a sense of despair. But in the in the same time, the Muslims were making this brand new Empire, they were filled with Vigor, they had this new religion, (the true religion in both Spiritually and Logic) there was hope, there were dreams, they encountered philosophy and they fell in love with it and they ran with it and so I think there was a little bit of that going on; Then Christians go oh my God! why do we burn all that and then they bring it back and the next thing you know Britain conquers 40 of the planet. And so there's this pendulum switch, and I gonna say I like one end of the swing. I do, I love science. I love things like antibiotics, antibiotics are wonderful. I love calculus, I think it's a great thing you should learn it. Physics, boundless love of physics, when that pendulum comes swinging back the other way and we're setting books on fire and pulling them out of libraries in Texas, it freaks me out, I've read about it anyway I wasn't there and I know how this story ends and you're not gonna like it, you're not we don't need to do this again. We've done it before, it wasn't great.

It wasn't great just for the record.

Chapter 10

Conclusion

Dr. Roy Casagranda shows how the so-called "Dark Ages" were actually a time of great intellectual achievement and challenges the artificial East-West paradigm. Dr. Casagranda looks at how Muslim Persian, Jewish, Christian, and Muslim Arab philosophers preserved and advanced Western civilization while Europe sank into the Medieval era, pointing out the contradictions in the construct of the western civilization paradigm.

Jorting Space